RAYS
Animals with an Electric Charge

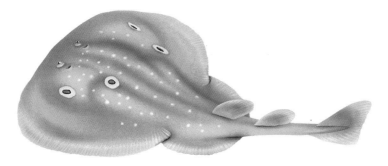

by Andreu Llamas
Illustrated by Gabriel Casadevall and Ali Garousi

Gareth Stevens Publishing
MILWAUKEE

For a free color catalog describing Gareth Stevens' list of high-quality books and multimedia programs, call 1-800-542-2595 (USA) or 1-800-461-9120 (Canada). Gareth Stevens Publishing's Fax: (414) 225-0377.
See our catalog, too, on the World Wide Web: http://gsinc.com

The editor would like to extend special thanks to Jan W. Rafert, Curator of Primates and Small Mammals, Milwaukee County Zoo, Milwaukee, Wisconsin, for his kind and professional help with the information in this book.

Library of Congress Cataloging-in-Publication Data

Llamas, Andreu.
    [Raya. English]
    Rays: animals with an electric charge / by Andreu Llamas ; illustrated by
Gabriel Casadevall and Ali Garousi.
        p. cm. – (Secrets of the animal world)
    Includes bibliographical references and index.
    Summary: Describes the physical characteristics, habitat, behavior, and life
cycle of these flat fish, some of which have organs that can produce electricity.
    ISBN 0-8368-1642-0 (lib. bdg.)
    1. Rays (Fishes)–Juvenile literature. [1. Rays (Fishes).] I. Casadevall,
Gabriel, ill. II. Garousi, Ali, ill. III. Title. IV. Series.
    QL638.8.L5313   1997
    597.3'5–dc21   97-8490

This North American edition first published in 1997 by
Gareth Stevens Publishing
1555 North RiverCenter Drive, Suite 201
Milwaukee, Wisconsin 53212 USA

This U.S. edition © 1997 by Gareth Stevens, Inc. Created with original © 1993
Ediciones Este, S.A., Barcelona, Spain. Additional end matter © 1997 by Gareth
Stevens, Inc.

Series editor: Patricia Lantier-Sampon
Editorial assistants: Diane Laska, Rita Reitci

Printed in the United States of America

1 2 3 4 5 6 7 8 9 01 00 99 98 97

CONTENTS

THE WORLD OF RAYS

Where rays live

About 470 species of Batoidea, or rays, exist today. These aquatic animals typically have short, flat bodies and long tails. Rays spend a lot of time half-buried in sand on the sea floor. They are related to sharks.

Several hundred species of fish have electric organs, but only a few can send out a strong discharge. Most of the electric fish in the sea are batoids, which live in tropical conditions at depths up to 9,845 feet (3,000 meters). Other species live in rivers and lakes.

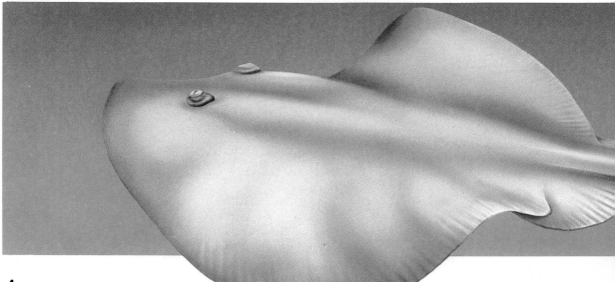

The different species of electric fish are found in all the seas and oceans of the world.

RAY	
ELECTRIC CATFISH	
ELECTRIC EEL	
MANTA	

Producers of electricity

Electricity-producing organs in fish are made of modified nerve and muscle cells. The South American electric eel and the electric ray, or torpedo, can send out the most powerful electric charges.

Other fish are sensitive to slight changes in the electric field around them. Rays can tell differences of only 0.01 microvolts per 0.4 inch (1 centimeter), making them the most sensitive of all animals to electricity.

The torpedo is an electric marine animal that can produce very dangerous electric discharges.

Rays look much different from all other fish.

Types of electric fish

When any new system evolves in nature that increases the chances of survival for the animal that has it, many species begin to evolve until they also obtain and perfect the system. In fish, there is only one efficient system for producing an electric organ — by changing nerve and muscle cells. Electric organs have evolved along six lines: (1) in rays, with a great number of species in saltwater and some in freshwater; (2) in torpedoes, or electric rays, which live in the sea close to the coasts, although they can exist several hundred

MORMYRID

ELECTRIC EEL

TORPEDO

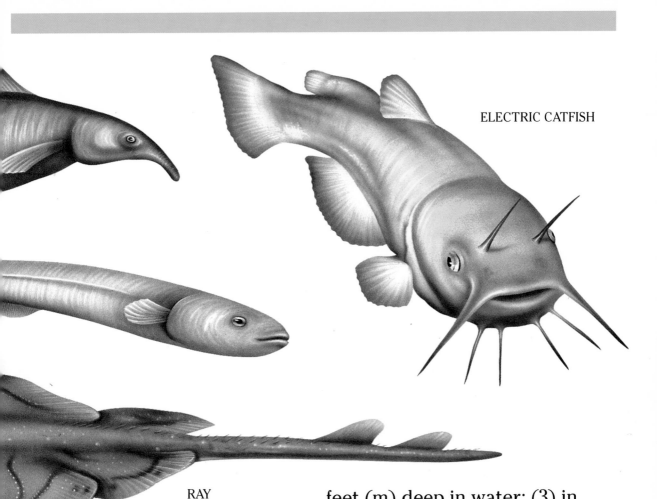

ELECTRIC CATFISH

RAY

URANOSCOPID

feet (m) deep in water; (3) in Mormyridae, about 120 species of fish that live in Africa's lakes and rivers; (4) in the electric catfish, which lives in the rivers of tropical Africa and that can discharge more than 300 volts; (5) in some Uranoscopidae, the only teleost, or bony, saltwater fish to have electric organs; (6) in the electric eel and Gymnotidae, or knife eels, that live in the rivers of Central and South America.

INSIDE THE RAY

Rays and torpedoes are adapted to life on the seabed. Their flat body can measure 6.5 feet (2 m) in many species. The fish have highly developed pectoral fins, which are joined to the head at the front. Because of this, most rays move through the water as if they are flying, using their fins like wings. Torpedoes, on the other hand, swim in a jerkier manner, using their tails to move them forward. The shape of their bodies and their way of moving make it easy for them to bury themselves in the sand at the bottom to find food or hide.

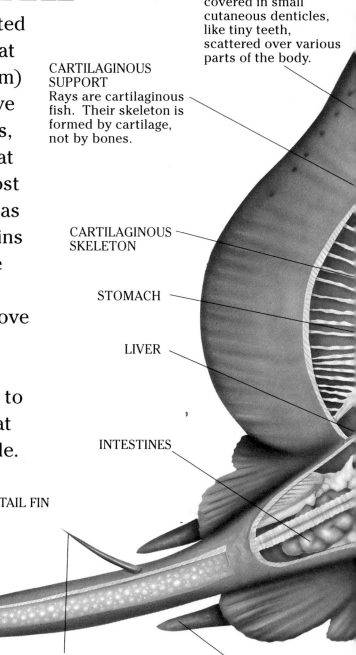

SKIN
The skin is rough and covered in small cutaneous denticles, like tiny teeth, scattered over various parts of the body.

CARTILAGINOUS SUPPORT
Rays are cartilaginous fish. Their skeleton is formed by cartilage, not by bones.

CARTILAGINOUS SKELETON

STOMACH

LIVER

INTESTINES

TAIL FIN

DORSAL FINS

TAIL
The tail is thin. At the end are two small dorsal fins and a tail fin that can also be very thin through lack of use.

POISONOUS SPINE
Some species may have one or more poisonous spines on the tail that are powerful weapons against enemies.

REPRODUCTIVE ORGAN

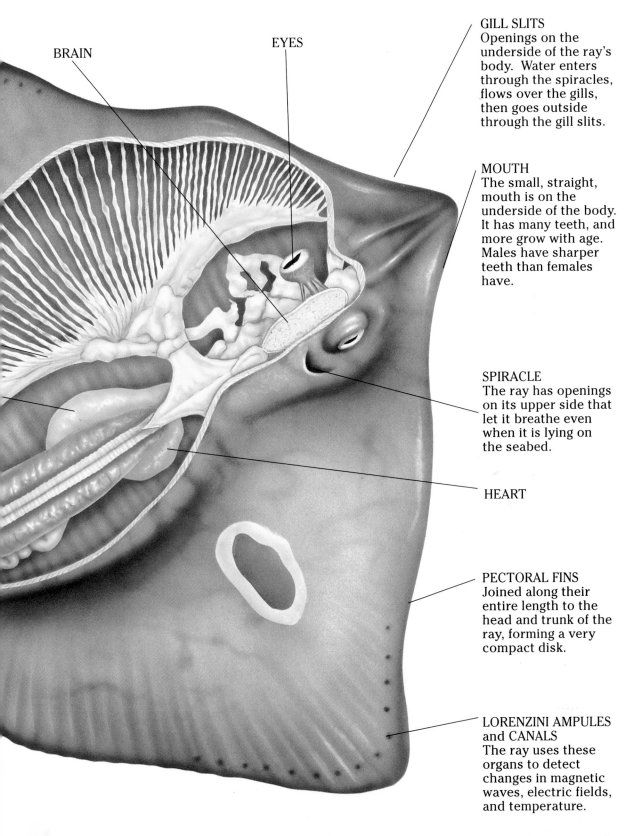

BRAIN

EYES

GILL SLITS
Openings on the
underside of the ray's
body. Water enters
through the spiracles,
flows over the gills,
then goes outside
through the gill slits.

MOUTH
The small, straight,
mouth is on the
underside of the body.
It has many teeth, and
more grow with age.
Males have sharper
teeth than females
have.

SPIRACLE
The ray has openings
on its upper side that
let it breathe even
when it is lying on
the seabed.

HEART

PECTORAL FINS
Joined along their
entire length to the
head and trunk of the
ray, forming a very
compact disk.

LORENZINI AMPULES
and **CANALS**
The ray uses these
organs to detect
changes in magnetic
waves, electric fields,
and temperature.

ANIMAL ELECTRICITY

Animal batteries

All animal cells can generate small electric charges. In some fish, special cells have evolved so that they can generate much larger electric charges. These cells came from nerve cells and from muscle cells that can no longer contract.

Electric organs vary widely in place and shape. The electric ray, or torpedo, has a gelatinous mass on each side of the head. They are made of small electric plates, or electroplates, stacked up to form columns. These columns are neatly arranged

The stacks of electroplates work like a battery.

A sting from a ray makes a deep wound.

Electrogenous organs, which are very large in the torpedo, receive a great number of nerves from the brain.

next to one another. Each plate is made of a special flattened cell. A message comes through the nerves to the fish's muscles to produce an electric charge.

Instantly, the voltage of all the electroplates combines to produce electric charges, from 220 volts in the torpedo up to 650 volts in the electric eel, strong enough to stun a human.

Electric plates in animals

Electric plates, or electroplates, in fish are disklike structures. One side is connected to nerve fibers, while the other is made up of many folds with lots of indentations. Electric organs have a clear, gelatinous appearance because the cells that form the organs are transparent. Each electroplate is covered with a gelatinous film. All plates usually face the same direction, stacked on top of one another in columns containing 150 or 200 plates. In the torpedo, there can be 140 to 1,000 electroplates in each column, and as many as half a million in a large torpedo.

Magnified image of two electroplates.

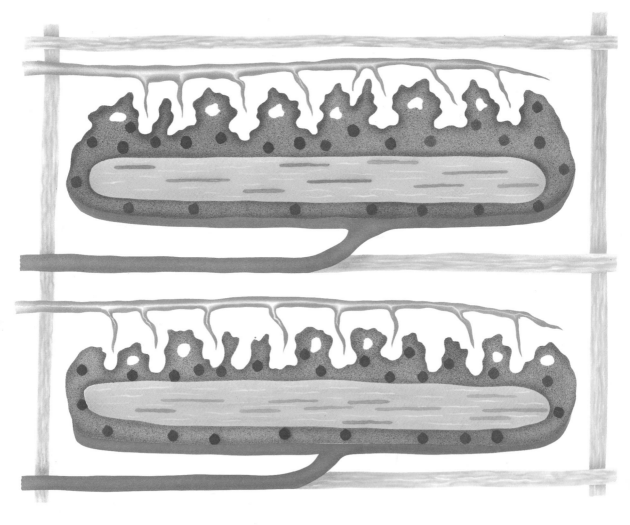

Location of electric organs

A torpedo's electric organs are at the base of its fins. Other species may have electroplates in other parts of the body. The electric eel has electroplates in two columns along the length of its underside and can send charges from head to tail. Rays and mormyrids have electric organs in the tail, producing only mild charges.

In some Uranoscopids, electric organs lie behind the eyes. In electric catfish, they are in the center of the body.

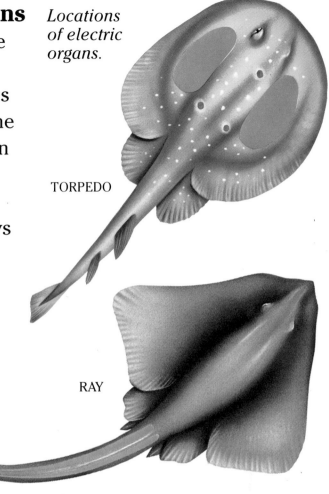

Locations of electric organs.

TORPEDO

RAY

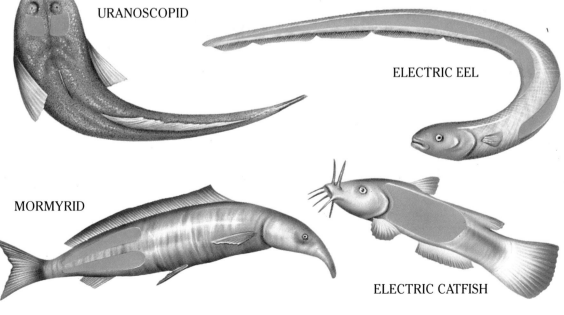

URANOSCOPID

ELECTRIC EEL

MORMYRID

ELECTRIC CATFISH

USING ELECTRICITY

Hunting and self-defense

Electric organs in fish began to evolve more than 400 million years ago. Over time, they have developed to make up half of the electric eel's body, with about seventy columns of plates on each side. Each column has between six thousand and ten thousand plates that together produce a high voltage. The ability to send out strong electric charges is a powerful and efficient defense mechanism against possible predators. It is also a good way to catch food with little effort.

Enlarged detail of a Lorenzini ampule.

NERVES

AMPULE

TUBE

EXTERNAL PORE

A torpedo catches fish using electric charges.

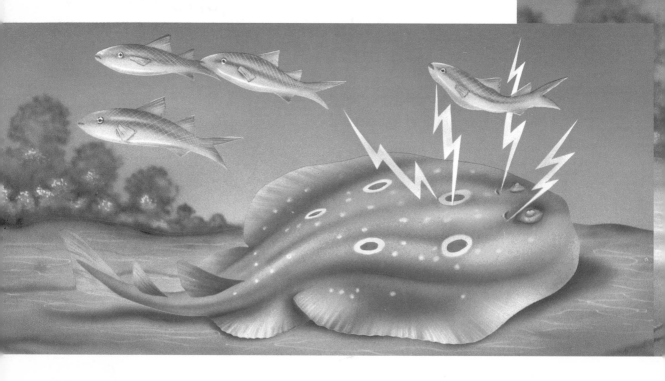

Torpedoes, for example, hide in the sand and produce charges to stun their prey. Then the torpedo wraps its body around the victim and devours it. It is possible to find fish of all kinds inside the torpedo's stomach.

Electric fish in the sea have an advantage. Electricity passes through saltwater more easily than through freshwater. This makes their charges more powerful and dangerous.

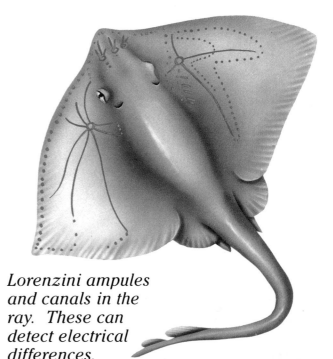

Lorenzini ampules and canals in the ray. These can detect electrical differences.

Electric fields to explore

Electric fish create waves of electric current in the water around them. To do this, they make small, rapid discharges, up to over a thousand per second. When something enters this electric field, it makes a change in the electric current that the fish can detect because of its sensitivity to electric differences. Electric fish can be 500,000 times more sensitive to electricity than non-electric fish. This ability is useful at night or in muddy waters where freshwater electric fish live.

With its electric field, a torpedo can tell the difference between an enemy and possible prey approaching.

that a manta can grow
up to 30 feet (9 m) wide?

Manta rays, or devilfish, live far above the seabed with the help of their highly developed fins. They can measure 30 feet (9 m) wide and weigh more than 4,400 pounds (2,000 kilograms).

In spite of its impressive size, the manta is not aggressive. It feeds on plankton that enters its mouth through two extensions on the head known as cephalic horns.

ANCESTORS OF THE RAYS

The first electric fish

Four hundred million years ago, the sea was already full of many different kinds of animals that needed protection from predators in order to survive. Over time, many species developed special defense systems. Hemicyclaspis, only a few inches (cm) long, evolved an unusual defense system on its head. This was a long, thin, electric organ that gave enemies a powerful electric shock.

Electric organs have been essential to the survival of Hemicyclaspis for a very long time.

Primitive rays

Spathobathis, the oldest known ray, lived more than 160 million years ago. Its body was about 20 inches (50 cm) long and had flattened to adapt to life on the sea floor. Its eyes and spiracles were on the top of its head. Grooves for the gills were on the underside. Its pectoral fins were in the same position as today's rays, and it swam with an undulating action of these fins. Its mouth was on the underside and contained wide, flat teeth to grind shells and crustaceans.

Spathobathis resembled the modern ray by the end of the Jurassic period.

Gemuendina, which lived 260 million years ago, was not an ancestor of the ray but had many of its characteristics.

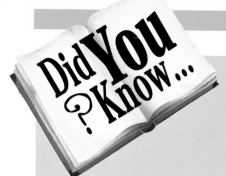

that there are freshwater rays?

Freshwater rays are one of the few groups of cartilaginous fish that live in lakes and rivers, mostly in South America and tropical Africa. These rays have a tail armed with two long, pointed spines that have serrated edges connected to poisonous glands. Humans living in these regions are careful to avoid disturbing these rays. If they do, the victims may suffer a painful sting.

THE LIFE OF THE RAYS

Born in a capsule

All rays are oviparous. Young hatch already fully developed from rectangular, nearly transparent capsules. A filament from each corner of the capsule attaches it to seaweed.

When the ray leaves the egg, the empty capsule is carried along by the current and can wash up on beaches. These remains are sometimes called "mermaid's purses."

A large yolk sac inside the capsule nourishes the ray embryo.

A newly hatched ray looks just like a miniature adult.

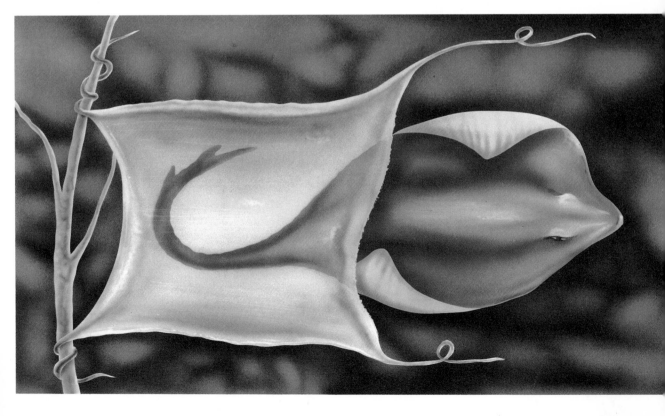

that sharks have electricity detectors, too?

Sharks also have a system, similar to the ray's, that can detect electric differences. Lorenzini ampules and canals are located under the skin of the shark's head and form a line, called the lateral line, down each side to the tail. The system stays in contact with the exterior through pores in the skin surface. Sharks use this sense to find their way over short distances, during migration, and for locating prey.

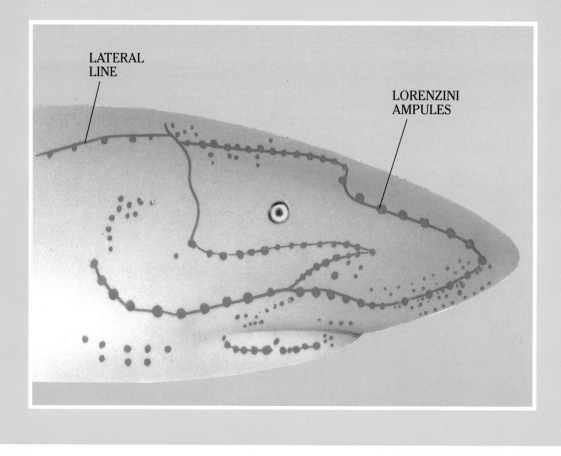

LATERAL
LINE

LORENZINI
AMPULES

Flying in the water

For the electrical field of electricity-producing marine creatures to work correctly, their generating and receiving organs must be lined up. To keep their electric organs in line down the length of their bodies, electric fish hold themselves rigid when swimming.

Rays move with an up-and-down undulating motion from head to tail. They move their pectoral fins like a bird's wings, making it look as though the fish is flying under water.

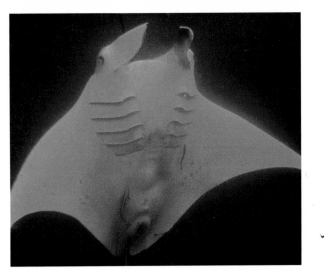

From underneath, the manta looks like an enormous glider.

How the common ray moves its fins when swimming.

APPENDIX TO

SECRETS
OF THE
ANIMAL WORLD

RAYS
Animals with an Electric Charge

RAY SECRETS

Electric barriers. Scientists in South Africa, knowing that sharks and other fish are affected by electric fields, are trying to develop a system to protect bathers on the beaches from these dangerous fish.

▼ The most powerful charge. The fish with the strongest electric charge is the electric eel, which can produce up to

650 volts. This amount of electricity is extremely dangerous for even very large mammals.

▼ The elegant ray. One species of ray is called the "marine eagle" because of the majestic undulatory motion of its pectoral fins. It has a poisonous spine in the middle of its tail to use against enemies.

▼ Using the ray. Some tribes use the ray's parts to make spearheads, whips, and drums.

Greedy eaters. When an electric fish is put into an aquarium, it uses its powerful electric charge to stun other fish and then devour them.

▶ **A special belly.** A ray's belly is easy to identify, since it spends most of its time on the seabed. Its pectoral fins are considered a delicacy, although in some species they smell like ammonia.

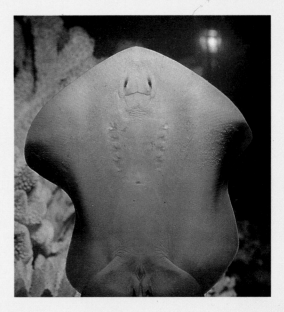

1. The electric eel lives in:
a) European lakes and rivers.
b) Central and South American rivers.
c) African lakes and rivers.

2. Torpedoes can emit charges of:
a) more than 100 volts.
b) more than 200 volts.
c) up to 650 volts.

3. The electric fish's sensitivity to electricity is:
a) up to 1,000 times greater than non-electric fish.
b) less than that of non-electric fish.
c) up to 500,000 times greater than that of non-electric fish.

4. The oxygen-containing water that the ray needs to breathe:
a) enters by the mouth and leaves by the spiracle.
b) enters by the spiracle and leaves by the gill slits.
c) enters by the gill slits and leaves by the mouth.

5. The manta can weigh:
a) more than 1,100 pounds (500 kg).
b) more than 4,400 lbs. (2,000 kg).
c) more than 26,450 lbs. (12,000 kg).

6. The oldest known ray is:
a) Spathobathis.
b) Hemicyclaspis.
c) Gemuendina.

The answers to RAY SECRETS questions are on page 32.

GLOSSARY

adapt: to make changes or adjustments in order to survive in a changing environment.

aggressive: bold; eager to challenge or engage in combat.

ampules of Lorenzini: a feature in the ray's body that enables it to sense weak electric fields. Electricity is detected through pores near the bottom of a ray's snout that lead to jelly-filled sacs known as the ampules of Lorenzini. All creatures have an electric field, so these sense organs help a ray find and follow its prey.

ancestors: previous generations of a family or species.

aquatic: living or growing in water.

capsule: a small container or compartment.

cartilage: an elastic substance that helps hold the bones in place at the joints. Rays, sharks, and skates have skeletons made of cartilage.

cephalic: referring to the head region of an animal.

characteristics: traits or features that separate, or identify, an object or organism from others.

contract (v): to pull up or draw together.

crustaceans: animals with a hard outer shell that live mostly in water. Crabs and lobsters are crustaceans.

current: a flowing mass of air or water; a flow of electricity.

cutaneous denticles: conelike pointed projections, like small teeth, in the skin of rays and sharks.

devour: to eat hungrily or greedily.

discharge: the release of an amount of electricity.

efficient: the ability to use something without waste. The ability to send out electric charges is an efficient defense mechanism against predators.

electric charge: a quantity of electricity, especially if it is stored in something.

electrogenous: the production of electric activity in living tissue.

electroplates: special cells of an animal that produce electricity, usually stacked in columns.

embryo: an animal in the very earliest stages of growth, usually in an egg.

emit: to send forth or give out.

essential: something that cannot be done without.

evolve: to change or develop gradually from one form to another. Over time, all living things must evolve to survive in their changing environments; otherwise, they may become extinct.

extensions: a part that sticks out from the main object or animal.

exterior: the outer surface.

filament: a fine, threadlike piece.

gelatinous: jellylike.

gills: the breathing organs in fish.

indentation: the part of a surface that is deeper than the rest, like a groove or pit.

marine: of or related to the sea.

migration: the moving from one place or climate to another, usually on a seasonal basis.

modified: something that is changed in a way that improves it or makes it more useful in another way.

organ: a group of tissues and cells in an animal or a plant that make up a structure that does special work.

oviparous: able to produce eggs that hatch outside the mother's body.

pectoral fins: fins that extend from the side of the body and help the ray swim and steer.

plankton: tiny plants and animals that drift in river, lake, and ocean waters. Plankton form an important food source for many marine animals.

pore: a tiny opening, especially in plant or animal skin.

predators: animals that kill and eat other animals.

prey: animals that are killed for food by other animals.

sensitive: easily affected by or made aware of something.

serrated: having a jagged or zigzag edge, like a steak knife.

species: animals or plants that are closely related and often similar in behavior and appearance. Members of the same species can breed together.

teleost: a fish with a skeleton made of bone.

transparent: allowing light to pass through so that objects on the inside or on the other side can be seen clearly.

tropical: belonging to the tropics, or the region centered on the equator and lying between the Tropic of Cancer (23.5 degrees north of the equator) and the Tropic of Capricorn (23.5 degrees south of the equator). This region is typically very hot and humid.

undulate: to move in a wavy or flowing manner.

voltage: measurement of electric power.

ACTIVITIES

◆ Compare the internal and external anatomy of rays with sharks. In what ways are these fish alike? How are they different? Do you think their anatomy has anything to do with how they act?

◆ Humans also produce bioelectricity, which can be measured in various organs by machines to help find disease. Look in library books about medical diagnosis and make a list of some of these machines and the organs, such as the heart, whose electric patterns they measure. Another machine, the lie detector, measures galvanic (electric) skin response. How does this help determine if a person is telling the truth or a lie? What other kinds of emotions could affect the machine?

◆ Rays and sharks make a good food source for humans in many parts of the world. Find out what non-food parts of these animals are also used. How does pollution and overfishing affect the survival of these animals? What can we do about this?

MORE BOOKS TO READ

Amazing Fish. Mary Ling (Knopf Books for Young Readers)
Colors of the Sea (5 vols.). Eric Ethan and M. Bearanger (Gareth Stevens)
Dangerous Fish. Ray Broekel (Childrens Press)
Dangerous Water Creatures. Michael Peissel (Chelsea House)
Fearsome Fish. Steve Parker (Raintree Steck-Vaughn)
Giants of the Deep. Q. L. Pearce (Lowell House)
Shark and Ray. Vincent Serventy (Raintree Steck-Vaughn)
Sharks and Other Creatures of the Deep. Phillip Steele
    (Dorling Kindersley)
Sharks, Rays, and Eels: Golden Junior Guide. Christopher Lampton
    (Golden Press)
Strange Animals of the Sea. Jerry Pinkney (National Geographic)
Under the Sea: Weird and Wonderful Creatures from the Deep. Leighton
    Taylor (Chronicle Books)
World's Weirdest Sea Creatures. M. L. Roberts (Troll Communications)

VIDEOS

Dolphins, Rays, and Other Adaptations. (Altschul Group)
Oceans Alive! Pt. 1 and Pt. 4. (Environmental Media)
The Ocean at Night: The Sea of Cortez. (Environmental Media)
Sharks and Rays. (Encyclopædia Britannica Educational Corporation)

PLACES TO VISIT

**National Aquarium in
    Baltimore**
Pier 3, 501 E. Pratt Street
Baltimore, MD 21202

Vancouver Aquarium
Stanley Park
West Georgia Avenue
Vancouver, B.C. V6B 3X8

Aquarium du Quebec
1675 Avenue des Hotels
Sainte-Foy, Quebec
G1W 4S3

**Kelly Tarleton's
    Underwater World**
Orakei Wharf, Tamaki Dr.
Auckland 1, New Zealand

Monterey Bay Aquarium
886 Cannery Row
Monterey Bay, CA 93940

**National Aquarium and
    Wildlife Sanctuary**
Lady Denman Drive
Canberra, NSW
Australia 2601

INDEX